First World War
and Army of Occupation
War Diary
France, Belgium and Germany

59 DIVISION
176 Infantry Brigade,
Brigade Trench Mortar Battery
17 February 1917 - 31 December 1918

WO95/3021/14

The Naval & Military Press Ltd
www.nmarchive.com
Published in association with The National Archives

Published by

The Naval & Military Press Ltd

Unit 10 Ridgewood Industrial Park,

Uckfield, East Sussex,

TN22 5QE England

Tel: +44 (0) 1825 749494

www.naval-military-press.com

www.nmarchive.com

This diary has been reprinted in facsimile from the original. Any imperfections are inevitably reproduced and the quality may fall short of modern type and cartographic standards.

© **Crown Copyright**
Images reproduced by permission of The National Archives, London, England, 2015.

Contents

Document type	Place/Title	Date From	Date To
Heading	WO95/3021/14		
Heading	59th Division 176th Infy Bde 176th Lt. Trench Mortar Bty Feb 1917-Dec 1918		
Heading	176th Light Trench Mortar Battery February To December 1917		
Miscellaneous	On His Majesty's Service.		
War Diary	Codford	19/02/1917	19/02/1917
War Diary	S'Hampton	19/02/1917	21/02/1917
War Diary	At Sea	22/02/1917	22/02/1917
War Diary	Havre	23/02/1917	23/02/1917
War Diary	Longeau	24/02/1917	24/02/1917
War Diary	Glisy	25/02/1917	25/02/1917
War Diary	Hamel	26/02/1917	26/02/1917
War Diary	Moor Court	27/02/1917	28/02/1917
War Diary	Fovant	17/02/1917	17/02/1917
War Diary	S/Hampton Water	18/02/1917	20/02/1917
War Diary	Havre	21/02/1917	22/02/1917
War Diary	Longeau	23/02/1917	25/02/1917
War Diary	Bayon-Villers	26/02/1917	28/02/1917
Heading	War Diary of 176th Light French Mortar Battery From 1st March 1917 To 29th March 1917		
War Diary	Moor Court	01/03/1917	04/03/1917
War Diary	Foucaucourt	05/03/1917	06/03/1917
War Diary	In The Field	07/03/1917	29/03/1917
Heading	War Diary of 176th Light Trench Mortar Battery From 30th March 1917 To 30th April 1917		
War Diary	In The Field	30/03/1917	30/04/1917
Heading	War Diary of 176th Light Trench Mortar Battery From 1st May 1917 To 31st May 1917		
War Diary	2 19.d.3 1/2-1 1/2 In The Field	01/05/1917	10/05/1917
War Diary	In The Field	11/05/1917	31/05/1917
Miscellaneous	Headquarters 59th Division	09/07/1917	09/07/1917
Heading	War Diary of 176th Light Trench Mortar Battery From 1st June 1917 To 30th June 1917		
War Diary	In The Field	01/06/1917	30/06/1917
Heading	War Diary of 176th Light Trench Mortar Battery From 1st July 1917 To 31st July 1917		
War Diary	In The Field	01/07/1917	31/07/1917
Heading	War Diary of 176th Light Trench Mortar Battery From 1st Aug 1917 To 31st Aug 1917		
War Diary	In The Field	01/08/1917	31/08/1917
Heading	War Diary of 176th Light Trench Mortar Battery From Sept 1st 1917 To Sept 30th 1917		
War Diary	Winnezeele	01/09/1917	19/09/1917
War Diary	Brandhoek	20/09/1917	21/09/1917
War Diary	Goldfish Chateau	22/09/1917	25/09/1917
War Diary	Wieltje	26/09/1917	28/09/1917
War Diary	Vlamertinghe	29/09/1917	29/09/1917
War Diary	Trappistes Camp	30/09/1917	30/09/1917

Heading	War Diary of 176th Light Trench Mortar Battery From 1st Oct 1917 To 31st Oct 1917		
War Diary	Trappistes Camp	01/10/1917	01/10/1917
War Diary	In The Field	02/10/1917	31/10/1917
Heading	War Diary of 176th Trench Mortar Battery From 1st Nov 1917 To 30th Nov 1917		
War Diary	In The Field	01/11/1917	30/11/1917
Heading	War Diary of 176th Light Trench Mortar Battery From 1st Dec 1917 To 31st Dec 1917		
War Diary	In The Field	01/12/1917	31/12/1917
Heading	War Diary of 176th Light Trench Mortar Battery From 1st Jun 1918 To 31st Jun 1918		
War Diary	In The Field	01/01/1918	31/01/1918
Heading	War Diary of 176th Light Trench Mortar Battery From 1st Feby 1918 To 28th Feby 1918		
War Diary	In The Field	01/02/1918	28/02/1918
Heading	War Diary of 176th Light Trench Mortar Battery From 1st March 1918 To 31st March 1918		
War Diary	In The Field	01/03/1918	31/03/1918
Heading	176th Brigade 59th Division 176th Brigade Light Trench Mortar Battery April 1918		
Heading	War Diary of 176th Light Trench Mortar Battery From 1st April 1918 To 30th April 1918		
War Diary	In The Field	01/04/1918	30/04/1918
Heading	War Diary of 176 Trench Mortar Battery From July 1st 1918 To July 31st 1918 Volume I		
War Diary	Hestrus	11/07/1918	11/07/1918
War Diary	Guernonval	12/07/1918	23/07/1918
War Diary	Bretencourt	24/07/1918	31/07/1918
Heading	War Diary of 176th Trench Mortar Battery From 1.8.18 To 31.8.18 Volume II		
War Diary	Blaireville Mercatel Sector	01/08/1918	04/08/1918
War Diary	Barly	05/08/1918	07/08/1918
War Diary	Blairville Mercatel Sector	08/08/1918	26/08/1918
War Diary	Hamet Billets	27/08/1918	31/08/1918
Heading	War Diary of 176 Light Trench Mortar Battery From 1-9-18 To 30-9-18 Volume III		
War Diary	Asylum St. Venant	01/09/1918	03/09/1918
War Diary	Calonne	04/09/1918	08/09/1918
War Diary	Lestrem	09/09/1918	30/09/1918
Heading	War Diary 176 L.T.M.B. From 1st Oct To 31st Oct 1918		
War Diary	Laventie	01/10/1918	02/10/1918
War Diary	Sailly-Sur-La Lys	03/10/1918	09/10/1918
War Diary	Armentieres Front	10/10/1918	17/10/1918
War Diary	Lille	17/10/1918	19/10/1918
War Diary	Chaos	20/10/1918	21/10/1918
War Diary	Templeuve	22/10/1918	31/10/1918
Heading	War Diary 176 L.T.M.B. From 1st November To 30th November 1918		
War Diary	Toufflers	01/11/1918	08/11/1918
War Diary	Templeuve	09/11/1918	09/11/1918
War Diary	St Aubert	09/11/1918	10/11/1918
War Diary	Velaines	10/11/1918	12/11/1918
War Diary	St Aubert	12/11/1918	15/11/1918
War Diary	Willems	15/11/1918	16/11/1918

War Diary	Lille	16/11/1918	30/11/1918
Heading	War Diary 176 L.T.M.B. From 1st Dec 1918 To 31 Dec 1918		
War Diary	Lille	01/12/1918	06/12/1918
War Diary	Barlin	06/12/1918	31/12/1918

005/3021/14

59TH DIVISION
176TH INFY BDE

176TH LT. TRENCH MORTAR BTY
FEB 1917-DEC 1918

176th Light Trench
Mortar Battery

February to December 1917

On His Majesty's Service.

An Darcey Esq.
Dist. deel.
6/80
Audit House.
Vic Encl
Vic Jcy.

WAR DIARY
INTELLIGENCE SUMMARY
(Erase heading not required.)

Army Form C. 2118.

T M Bty c

Vol 1 / 11

Instructions regarding War Diaries and Intelligence Summaries are contained in F.S. Regs., Part II. and the Staff Manual respectively. Title Pages will be prepared in manuscript.

Place	Date	Hour	Summary of Events and Information	Remarks and references to Appendices
Eastport	19/2/17	10.40 PM	Entrained for Southampton	
S'HAMPTON	19/2/17	4 P.M.	SPENT NIGHT IN REST. CAMP.	
do	20/2/17		Remained all day in Southampton Docks	
do	21/2/17	2.30 AM	EMBARKED on S.S. "ARCHIMEDES."	
AT SEA	22/2/17		ALL DAY AT SEA. Anchored outside HAVRE at night	
HAVRE	23/2/17	10 AM	Disembarked at HAVRE and left for train at 3 P.M.	
LONGEAU	24/2/17	6 AM	Detrained and marched to CLISY and billeted overnight	
CLISY	25/2/17	10 AM	Marched by road to HAMEL and billeted overnight	
HAMEL	26/2/17	11 AM	Marched by road to MOOR COURT	
MOOR COURT	27/2/17		In Huts at MOORCOURT served as forward training	
do	28/2/17		Battery and transport	

Army Form C. 2118.

WAR DIARY
of 1/7th Infantry Battalion, 172nd Infantry Bde.
INTELLIGENCE SUMMARY
February 1917

(Erase heading not required.)

Instructions regarding War Diaries and Intelligence Summaries are contained in F. S. Regs., Part II. and the Staff Manual respectively. Title Pages will be prepared in manuscript.

S 2 cmk

Place	Date	Hour	Summary of Events and Information	Remarks and references to Appendices
France	Feb 17		Left for embarkation 6.11.34. Embarked on S.S. Huntscraft at Southampton	
S/HAMPTON WATER	Feb 18 19 20	16?	On board S.S. Huntscraft	
HAVRE	—	21	Disembarked after transport had run aground — Battn. taken off in a H.T.S. Proceeded by Route March to No 1 Rest Camp T.R.D. No 22 — Continued	
	—	22	Detrained — billeted at Longeau	
LONGEAU	—	23	Rested	
	—	24	Proceeded by Route March to Bayon-Villers	
	—	25	Rested at Bayon-Villers. Capt. C. Gaudy M.27 a 8.9 Shell frame. Battn proceeded by W.D.M.R. 145 style — Battn train	
BAYON- VILLERS	—	26		
	—	27	Of Battn proceeded attacked to Bayon-Villers	
	—	28	B & C S.W. attacked at Bayon-Villers Battn from	J.C. Howard Capt. Jas. Adjt. 1/M Rifles 17th Sept 17

Army Form C. 2118.

WAR DIARY
or
INTELLIGENCE SUMMARY

(Erase heading not required.)

Original

Instructions regarding War Diaries and Intelligence Summaries are contained in F. S. Regs., Part II. and the Staff Manual respectively. Title Pages will be prepared in manuscript.

Vol.

Confidential

War Diary

of

176th Light Trench Mortar Battery

From 1st March 1917

To 29th March 1917.

Place	Date	Hour	Summary of Events and Information	Remarks and references to Appendices

WAR DIARY
INTELLIGENCE SUMMARY

(Erase heading not required.)

Army Form C. 2118.

Instructions regarding War Diaries and Intelligence Summaries are contained in F. S. Regs., Part II. and the Staff Manual respectively. Title pages will be prepared in manuscript.

Place	Date	Hour	Summary of Events and Information	Remarks and references to Appendices
Moascar	1/3/17	8.30am	Capt Hampton Commanding "Book Section" to line up 151st Brigade Mortar Batty. Duties at that were rest of Batty remained carrying out	
"	2/3/17		General Training carried out	
"	3/3/17	3.30PM	2/Lt Lane Roberts and 10 O.R. proceeded to Ferncourt on Reporte to O/C 151st T.M.B. Rest of remainder of Battery and staff transported to Ferncourt arr 3/3/17 10am and 10 OR	
"	4/3/17		Remainder of Battery and staff transported to Ferncourt arr 3/3/17 10am with 151 T.M.B.	
Ferncourt	5/3/17		Rest of Morning spent on instruction with 151 T.M.B. Ordinary Gun exercise States etc	
"	6/3/17	10PM	Six Guns + detachments taken up to Brigade line in relief of same No. of 151st George Mortar Batty	
"			Guns reported in Trouble. Enemy Activity quiet	
2nd Trench	7/3/17		No enemy movement or aeroplanes and ammunition details at etc.	
"	8/3/17		Enemy Activity quiet	
"	9/3/17		Dispo g emplacements of enemy shells snipper Ref No. 1 Gun Mine 15.00 and 22.00 PM Enemy Trenches, Mittag and Snipers Key Actif Firing Ke 2nd Lt Who at Gordon Mortar in eye in Quarry Left Section 10 PM was RTO duty carrying Batty slightly wounded Guns Calibrated test inspection Samples of Bugler and Kenney	
"	10/3/17		from Enemy lines at 7am splinter of shot thros of M.G. from	

W. Hampton Capt
O.C. 151 T. M. B34

Army Form C. 2118.

WAR DIARY
or
INTELLIGENCE SUMMARY
(Erase heading not required.)

Instructions regarding War Diaries and Intelligence Summaries are contained in F. S. Regs., Part II. and the Staff Manual respectively. Title pages will be prepared in manuscript.

Place	Date	Hour	Summary of Events and Information	Remarks and references to Appendices
24th July	17/3/17		Sapper entered Amount period a number heavily Enemy quiet but wire cut start to from 6pm to 6am. Cleared and oiled Rifles	
	18/3/17		our Gas Helmets inspected. Our movement TMs active. Post in the	
			Cleared and Oiled Ammunition. Post Inspected. Exams T. B and Rifle Grenade. Active Out Artillery action at Dusk	
	14/3/17		Most attention in the big Out. Take Cos Alarm German Bombs on	
			Ripe Active Post Inspection	
	15/4/17		Enemies digging and improving their emplacement. Enemy clamorous October at	
	16/3/17		Relayed of C in C. New Emplacement No1. Snipers at Post at 16 Pt	
	17/3/17		overnight. Lots of animals OK Post Inspected. Enemy activity quiet	
			Or 7 Am. 8 Respuer Gun No1 Gun. 15 from No1 am. 18 from No3 in cooperation	
			with several Offensive. Enemy line found to have this expanded	
	18/3/17		Enemy action all quiet. All work another's Machine	
			a lot 10 top in daylight. No enemy .	
	19/3/17		Gas old and cleaner. Rifles . So Administration etc	
	20/3/17		Post in old in Att Mats. Rifles inspected	
	21/3/17		Arms items Sought upt. 9 Q. T.M.B. School. Not Carried at	

W. Rylands Cpl T. M. 13 Bth

Army Form C. 2118.

WAR DIARY
INTELLIGENCE SUMMARY
(Erase heading not required.)

Instructions regarding War Diaries and Intelligence Summaries are contained in F. S. Regs., Part II. and the Staff Manual respectively. Title pages will be prepared in manuscript.

Place	Date	Hour	Summary of Events and Information	Remarks and references to Appendices
In the field	21/3/17		Reconnoitred new front Headquarters and new dug outs at Villers Cotterets near 500x NE Muguwart	
	22/3/17		Dugout commenced on alternative Cavers Gun Emplacement with a new magazine about three bays	
			9/11 A.T. Relief Carried report for Battalion O/C N Staff	
	23/3/17		Sent Sonnester for B'ty not K.T.M.B.	
			Rifles, Sus silents and gun return despatched	
	24/3/17		2 Gun Carriage Wheels examined from Cavan Gun Emplacement	
			also Ammunition weather	
	25/3/17		Dugout continued a Cavers Gun Emplacement at an advance of six	
			2 New not No for fort Rifle ett inspection	
	26/3/17		All Stokes and Guns ammunition Headquarters T II A & B 9	
	27/3/17		Battery Dugging around old camp and expecting rain	
			New fatigue party 10/H at 4.00 for Root repairing	
	28/3/17 10 am		Move from rest stables to new Headquarters N. W A & B at Villers Cotterets	
	29/3/17		Day's work to be put in at New T.M.B. under Lieut Pratt, arrive also afternoon inspection parties for Stores/Dugout with a view to future improvements	
	am 30/3			

J.R. Hempenel Capt
176 T.M. Bty

A6945. Wt. W14422/M1160 350,000 12/16 D.D. & L. Forms/C/2118/14.

Army Form C. 2118.

WAR DIARY
or
INTELLIGENCE SUMMARY
(Erase heading not required.)

Original

War Diary

of

146th Light Trench Mortar Battery

From :- 30th March, 1917.

To :- 30th April, 1917.

Confidential

Army Form C. 2118.

WAR DIARY
or
INTELLIGENCE SUMMARY.
(Erase heading not required.)

Instructions regarding War Diaries and Intelligence Summaries are contained in F. S. Regs., Part II. and the Staff Manual respectively. Title pages will be prepared in manuscript.

Place	Date	Hour	Summary of Events and Information	Remarks and references to Appendices
In field	30/3/14	6 am	Reconnoitred right sector and looked at emplacements for 3 gun for defence of bridgers at BRIE	
	31/3/14		Reconnoitred left sector and found that 5 guns could be commanded by Rifle & M.G fire to the front of the sector. Only one commands all 6 guns in Right Sector and 3 more. Reconnoitred an extracts all 6 guns in Right Sector and 3 more emplacements marked out	
	1/4/17		Digging emplacements. Church Services in hits of N.C.O. Lookouts.	
	2/4/17		Digging emplacements	
	3/4/17		General training & Refitting	
	4/4/17		Stores & Personnel moved from BRIE to MONS-EN-CHAUSSEE	
	5/4/17		General Training	
	6/4/17		Left Half Batty moved to BERNES (RIGHT HALF BATTY not moved)	
	7/4/17		General training	
	8/4/17		Capt Kempsted reconnoitred ground round LE VERGUIER. Report filed	
			Batty joined H.Q. at BERNES.	
	9/4/17		4 guns + ammunition placed in JEANCOURT (L.26. D.2.22)	

Army Form C. 2118.

WAR DIARY
or
INTELLIGENCE SUMMARY.
(Erase heading not required.)

Instructions regarding War Diaries and Intelligence Summaries are contained in F. S. Regs., Part II. and the Staff Manual respectively. Title pages will be prepared in manuscript.

Place	Date	Hour	Summary of Events and Information	Remarks and references to Appendices
In the field	10/4/17		General training	
	11/4/17		Route Wien from ESTREE-EN-CHAUSSEE to BERNES ambulance wagon	
			personnel from BERNES to SUGAR FACTORY (16th D.O.4.)	
	12/4/17		Batt. Employed reconnoitred ground for gun emplacements	
	13/4/17		4 Emplacements commenced in Antelope left front	
	14/4/17		Gun emplacement selected at R.34 c. 6. 7	
	15/4/17		Personnel used to Neut. repairing at TEANCOURT	
	16/4/17		Practice with dummy Walk and instruction to Reserve Battery men	
	17/4/17		Road repairing. Spring practice	
	18/4/17		Reconnoitred right sub-sector and 3 gun emplacements sited	
	19/4/17		Road repairing and general training	
	20/4/17		Road repairing and Church Parade	
	21/4/17		Road repairing and Battery drill etc	
	22/4/17		General training & road repairing	
	24/4/17		Road repairing & Battery drill	
	25/4/17		Road repairing & general training	

Army Form C. 2118.

WAR DIARY
or
INTELLIGENCE SUMMARY.
(Erase heading not required.)

Place	Date	Hour	Summary of Events and Information	Remarks and references to Appendices
Intpeny	24/4/19		Batt-y still at Roupy quarry	
	28/4/19		Gunr Personnel move from SUGAR FACTORY to FLECHIN. Gun not 177 L.T.M.B take over hills at SUGAR FACTORY	
	29/4/19		Sanitary arrangements made safer adequate cleaned away	
			Guns billets at FLECHIN	
	29/4/19		Guns stores & Personnel moved to VRAIGNES.	

Rampling Capt
O.C. 176 Light Trench Mortar Bt-ty

Army Form C. 2118.

WAR DIARY
INTELLIGENCE SUMMARY
(Erase heading not required.)

Confidential

War Diary
of
176th Light Trench Mortar Battery

From :- 1st May. 1917.
To :- 31st May. 1917.

Original

WAR DIARY or INTELLIGENCE SUMMARY

Army Form C. 2118.

Place	Date	Hour	Summary of Events and Information	Remarks and references to Appendices
2.19˚d.3.1.6 Jolyfield	1/5/17		Information is bad at VRAIGNES carried out. Snelled	
	2/5/17		Inspection by Brigade Commander. Firing dummies	
	3/5/17		Training to programme	
	4/5/17		Training do	
	5/5/17		Left Hempsread reconnoitred new line. Left Brigade General Training.	
	6/5/17		Battery & Stores moved to HESBECOURT. Relieved 148 L.T.M.B. H2 established at L.10.A.35. 3 Guns in Left Sector registered on Targets. One Gun on Right Sector registered on COLOGNE FARM.	
	7/5/17		One Sgt. Slightly wounded. New Emplacement dug on Left Sector for N°2 Gun. Shelters made for Ammunition.	
	8/5/17		Carried out Operation Orders dated 8/5/17. Hostile T.M. active Also Snipers. Enemy Dispersed by Guns	
	9/5/17		fire in front of MALAKOFF FARM.	

Army Form C. 2118.

WAR DIARY
INTELLIGENCE SUMMARY.
(Erase heading not required.)

Instructions regarding War Diaries and Intelligence Summaries are contained in F. S. Regs., Part II. and the Staff Manual respectively. Title pages will be prepared in manuscript.

Place	Date	Hour	Summary of Events and Information	Remarks and references to Appendices
In the field	11/5/17		Work carried on on New Emplacements. Heavy shelled by Heavy gun all forenoon. New Emplacement considered in Quarry.	
"	12/5/17		Progress made with New Emplacements	
"	13/5/17		Lt. Yockett dangerously wounded. Pte Ball slightly wounded by Shrapnel in Quarry. Work on New Emplacements continued	
	14/5/17		Quarry shelled during the day by 5.9. Night Quiet. Consolidation of positions proceeded with	
	15/5/17		Two Gun Emplacements completed. Right Sector No 2 Gun removed to New Position on left sector & Registered on Target.	
	16/5/17		Enemy activity quiet. No 1 Gun removed to New Emplacement on Left Sector & Registered on Target.	
	17/5/17		Nothing of importance to Record	
	18/5/17		Work of Improvement continued. Otherwise all quiet	
	9/5/17		A few rounds Shell fire Quarry in retaliation for our Trench Bombs	

WAR DIARY

~~INTELLIGENCE SUMMARY~~

(Erase heading not required.)

Army Form C. 2118.

Instructions regarding War Diaries and Intelligence Summaries are contained in F. S. Regs., Part II. and the Staff Manual respectively. Title pages will be prepared in manuscript.

Place	Date	Hour	Summary of Events and Information	Remarks and references to Appendices
In the field	20/5/17		Nothing of importance to record.	
	21/5/17		Left detd. party of enemy dispersed by gun fire close to Enfilade Trench.	
	22/6/17		Relieved by 174 L.T.M.B. No. 2 removed to L.63 a 24.	
	23/5/17		Guns cleaned & overhauled & stores checked	
	24/5/17		Battery proceeded to VAUX-en-AMIENOIS on course. Billetted for night in PERONNE.	
	25/5/17		Left PERONNE. 10.30am. Arrived AMIEN 3.P.M.	
	26/5/17		Drill & Instruction on course.	
	27/5/17		do	
	28/5/17		do	
	29/5/17		do	
	30/5/17		do	
	31/5/17		do	

Rawlett
for O.C. 146 L.T.M.B.

CONFIDENTIAL.

Headquartes,
    59th Division.

      Herewith original copy of War Diary for the month of June, for 176th Light Trench Mortar Battery.

9..7..17.
                              Brig. Genl.
                Commanding 176th Infantry Brigade.

Army Form C. 2118.

WAR DIARY
or
INTELLIGENCE SUMMARY

(Erase heading not required.)

Original

War Diary

of

146th Light Trench Mortar Battery

From: 1st June 1917
To: 30th June 1917

Confidential

Army Form C. 2118.

176TH LIGHT TRENCH MORTAR BATTERY.

WAR DIARY
or
INTELLIGENCE SUMMARY.
(Erase heading not required.)

Instructions regarding War Diaries and Intelligence Summaries are contained in F. S. Regs., Part II. and the Staff Manual respectively. Title pages will be prepared in manuscript.

Place	Date	Hour	Summary of Events and Information	Remarks and references to Appendices
In the Field	1/6/17		Seventh day of instruction of full battery at 4th Army School of Mortars, AMIENS	
	2/6/17		Eighth " " " " " " " " " "	
	3/6/17		Ninth " " " " " " " " " "	
	4/6/17		Tenth " " " " " " " " " "	
	5/6/17		Guns and Personnel moved from AMIENS to PERONNE	
	6/6/17		" " " " PERONNE to FINS (V. to G.8.2)	
	7/6/17		Training as per programme	
	8/6/17		do	
	9/6/17		do	
	10/6/17		do	
	11/6/17		Guns and Personnel moved from EQUANCOURT to METZ-EN-COUTURE 176th LTMB relieved at 8.30 PM 61st Bde Brigade front in front of BEAUCAMP	
	12/6/17		Guns and Personnel withdrawn from front line at 9.30 PM owing to enemy fire out of range	
	13/6/17		Fatigue Party supplied for work on No.4 C.T. under RE supervision	
	14/6/17		do	

Army Form C. 2118.

176TH LIGHT TRENCH MORTAR BATTERY.

No. ....
Date ....

WAR DIARY
or
INTELLIGENCE SUMMARY.
(Erase heading not required.)

Place	Date	Hour	Summary of Events and Information	Remarks and references to Appendices
In the Field	16/4/1		Battery moved to HARGICOURT in relief of 144th L.T.M.B. coming under command of 4th Dismounted Cavalry Brigade. Battery H.Q. L.10.a Central.	
	17th		General bombardments to surface of enemy line leaving the enemy left-up.	
	24th		from five guns on Rifle Pit-trench, Piccadilly Circus, New Year & Cologne trench.	
	27th		Barrage put down from four guns on Left-Sub-Sector a Rifle Pit, & Left & New trenches,	
	28th		in support of tapping raid by C.L.H. on Piccadilly Circus.	
	29th		No 2 Gun struck by a shell and knocked out in emplacement, no of left alley.	
	30th		kept in quarry. No casualties sustained. Work in new emplacement continued in preparation for resuming raid on	
			COLOGNE FARM	

R. Oswal Lieut
OC 67 Sec od
176 Lt M.B.
176 Light Mortar Battery

Army Form C. 2118.

WAR DIARY
or
INTELLIGENCE SUMMARY

(Erase heading not required.)

Place	Date	Hour	Summary of Events and Information	Remarks and references to Appendices
Original			War Diary of 146th Light Trench Mortar Battery From 1st July 1917 1. – 31st July 1917	Confidential

Instructions regarding War Diaries and Intelligence Summaries are contained in F. S. Regs., Part II. and the Staff Manual respectively. Title Pages will be prepared in manuscript.

Army Form C. 2118.

WAR DIARY
or
INTELLIGENCE SUMMARY.
(Erase heading not required.)

Instructions regarding War Diaries and Intelligence Summaries are contained in F. S. Regs., Part II. and the Staff Manual respectively. Title pages will be prepared in manuscript.

Place	Date	Hour	Summary of Events and Information	Remarks and references to Appendices
In Field	1/4/17		The Battery consisted of Artillery, horses & personnel for a raid on COLOGNE FARM, in which four Officers and one hundred and twenty other ranks took part.	651 Shells fired in 8 minutes
	2/4/17		Captain Thompson proceeded to Leave	
	3/4/17			
	4/4/17		New defensive emplacements dug for four guns at L.5.b.4.0.3 L.5.d.5.9.5	
	5/4/17		L.5.d.5-6 and L.5.d.3-3 respectively.	
	6/4/17			Taking over
	7/4/17		Sergeant and four men from 102nd T.M.B. gazetted up line for instruction of instructor.	
	8/4/17		Battery went to Ytreshem and stayed night owing to non-arrival of G.S. wagons to move stores etc. to ROISEL	
	9/4/17		Battery moved to training area at HARLINCOURT (O9.C.O.4)	
	10/4/17		Gun stores broken to this extent & cleaned. Battery having commenced	
	11th		Training as per programme. Box Respirators received by Divisional Gas N.C.O	
	12th		do	
	13th		do	
	14th		do	
	15/4/17 10 a.m.		Church Parade	
	16/4/17		Training as per programme	

Army Form C. 2118.

WAR DIARY
or
INTELLIGENCE SUMMARY.
(Erase heading not required.)

Instructions regarding War Diaries and Intelligence Summaries are contained in F. S. Regs., Part II. and the Staff Manual respectively. Title pages will be prepared in manuscript.

Place	Date	Hour	Summary of Events and Information	Remarks and references to Appendices
In the Field	17/4		Training as per programme	
	18/4		do	
	19/4		do	
	20/4		do	
	21/4		Capt'n Heywood returns from leave	
	22/4/17	10 am	Divisional Sports. No training after 11 AM	
	23/4/17		One officer and four other ranks proceeded to BOVES a course of French Mortar	
			Church Parade	
	24/4/17		Battery engaged in 176th Brigade Tactical Scheme No 1	
	25/4/17		Route march and Battery	
	26/4/17		Training as per programme	
			do	
	27/4/17		2/Lt Grice J.H. proceeded on leave	
			Battery engaged in 59th Divisional Tactical Scheme No 1	
	28/4/17		Training as per programme	
			Church Parade	
	29/4/17	10 am	Training as per programme	
	30/4/17		Battery engaged in 176th Brigade Tactical Scheme No 2	

W. Heywood Capt
176 T.M.B.

Army Form C. 2118.

WAR DIARY
or
INTELLIGENCE SUMMARY.
(Erase heading not required.)

Original   Confidential

War Diary

of

116th Light Trench Mortar Battery

From 1st Aug 1917
to 31st Aug 1917

Army Form C. 2118.

WAR DIARY
or
INTELLIGENCE SUMMARY.
(Erase heading not required.)

Instructions regarding War Diaries and Intelligence Summaries are contained in F. S. Regs., Part II. and the Staff Manual respectively. Title pages will be prepared in manuscript.

Place	Date	Hour	Summary of Events and Information	Remarks and references to Appendices
In the Field	1/8/19		Bad weather interferes with Div'l Tactical Exercise No 2 (without troops)	
	2/8/19		Battery engaged in digging drains for purposes of camp drainage.	
	3/8/19		Weather again prevents carrying out of Divisional Tactical Ex. No 2.	
	4/8/19		Training as per programme. 242126 Pt Beale AJ presented to BOYES as a cookery course	
	5/8/19	10.45AM	Training as per programme. Church Parade.	
	6/8/19		Divisional Field Day No 1. 2/Lt Stone P.J. Return from Course of Instruction at BOYES	
	7/8/19			
	8/8/19		Training as per programme	
	9/8/19		Training in morning. Demonstration (in 3 phases) of Infantry Battalions being present. 650 rounds fired.	
	10/8/19		Divisional Tactical Exercise No 3	
	11/8/19			
	12/8/19	10.15AM	Church Parade cancelled owing to inclement weather.	
	13/8/19		Brigade Sports	
	14/8/19		Training as per programme	
	15/8/19		Guns taken to Bapaume to be overhauled. Anti bluco placed on collars to prevent slipping.	
	16/8/19		Training during morning. Tents and wheat carried out in afternoon.	
	17/8/19		Practical camp cleaning in general respect (in view of parade tomorrow). Cleaning guns & equipment.	
	18/8/19		Orders:- 145/19 Battn of 2nd Armd 5 camp 9AM Gas school Tactical Ex.	

WAR DIARY
or
INTELLIGENCE SUMMARY.
(Erase heading not required.)

Army Form C. 2118.

Place	Date	Hour	Summary of Events and Information	Remarks and references to Appendices
In the Field	19/8/19	9.30-10.15AM	Bathing. 10.15AM Church Parade. Engineers Coy. taken over. B/C Hoisted. Proceeded to rest camp at VALERY-sur-SOMME. 242126 Pte Smith 29 returned from Courts of Sovres	
	29/8/19		Carrying party (10AM-5PM salt route) at 5 PM. Listrue to Officers, NCO's and Men by R.M.O. W.C. Full sharing as the treatment of. Guisthites by Bath. Gas NCO.	
	28/8/19		Training as per programme.	
	27/8/19		Battery moved to BUZINCOURT. Headquarters at NORTHUMBERLAND AVENUE Camp. at W.W.a Cent (Ref. ALBERT Contoured Sheet.)	
	24/8/19		Training as per programme.	
	25/8/19		" " "	
	26/8/19	11.30AM	Church Parade.	
	27/8/19		Training as per Programme	
	28/8/19		Preparation for move. 9PM move cancelled.	
	29/8/19			
	30/8/19	12.30PM	Training till 12.30PM. Preparations for move. 11.30PM Left BUZINCOURT.	
	31/8/19	1AM	1AM Entrained at AVELUY. 1PM Detrained at HOPOUTRE. Billeted at farmhouse at WINNEZEELE (Reference Contoured Sheet 34 (11 inch) T.18.6.9.	

W. Winford Capt
O.C. 146 T.M.B.

Original

Confidential

War Diary
of
176th Light Trench Mortar Battery

From Sept 1st 1917
to Sept 30th Oct 1917

Army Form C. 2118.

WAR DIARY
or
INTELLIGENCE SUMMARY.

(Erase heading not required.)

176th L.T.M.B.

Place	Date	Hour	Summary of Events and Information	Remarks and references to Appendices
WINNEZEELE	1/9/17	10 a.m.	Bttn Inspection. Foot do, Gas Mask do.	
	2/9/17		Church Parade	
	3/9/17		Bde Tactical Scheme	
	4/9/17		Training as per programme	
	5/9/17		" " " "	
	6/9/17		" " " "	
	7/9/17		" " " "	
	8/9/17		Church Parade	
	9/9/17		Bde Route March	
	10/9/17		Training as per programme	
	11/9/17		" " " "	
	12/9/17		" " " "	
	13/9/17		" " " "	
	14/9/17		Whole Holiday for Bde.	
	15/9/17		Church Parade	
	16/9/17		Bde Tactical Scheme	
	17/9/17		Training 2.00 p.m. Bde Jackdaw @ crossroads hear C.C.S. Mendingham. Bathing	
	18/9/17		Battalion Inspection. BRANDHOEK AREA BEDOUIN CAMP N17 WINNEZEELE 10.30 a.m. arrived dest. 5.30 p.m.	
	19/9/17		Physical exercises. Bn. No. 5 prepared any 10 more returned	
	20/9/17		Training, Cleaning it.	
BRANDHOEK	21/9/17	4.30 p.m.	6/176 Bedouin Camp M.H. (dismounted) at GOLDFISH CHATEAU at 5.45 P.M. Sheet 28 H.7.d.8.1	
	22/9/17		Remaining in Camp.	
GOLDFISH CHATEAU	23/9/17		Relieved 164th L.T.M.B. night of 23/24 4 x guns advanced to advanced B.H.Q. WIELTJE Sheet 28 C.18.b.2.6	
			Parties carrying toms up to O.R. under Mr Scott. SD Bonce S.A.A carried from BRIDGE HOUSE N. IBERIAN ST. POINT. 6 Casualties	
			Pte C.H. Fowler 1/6 W. South Staffs. Wounded. 20/910 Pte W. Perry 1/6 North Staffs. 17775 Pte F. Pellison 1/6 North Staffs. 240573	
			Pte Royd Park. 1/6 S.S. 203303 Pte L.A. Bromley 1/6 South Staffs. Artillery Relieved by 176 L.T.M.B. night	
			of 1/3/X. Half Battery of Gunners returned to GOLDFISH CHATEAU	
	1/9/17		Battery Guns moved up to B.H.Q. WIELTJE. H.Q. established in OXFORD ROAD	

Army Form C. 2118.

WAR DIARY
or
INTELLIGENCE SUMMARY.
(Erase heading not required.)

17b L.T.M.B

Place	Date	Hour	Summary of Events and Information	Remarks and references to Appendices
VIELTJE	26/4/17		Personal moved forward to CALL RESERVE. Patrols sent out to Nos. 5 & 6 Mortars.	
	27/4/17		1/60 rounds S.A.A. unloaded at BRIDGE HOUSE. Patrols on Nos. 5 & 6 Stokes. Personnel moved to Nos. 5 & 6.	
	28/4/17		Personnel moved back to VLAMERTINGHE	
VLAMERTINGHE	29/4/17		Heavy Stokes moved back to VLAMERTINGHE. Guns, Stores, Personnel moved to TRAPPISTES CAMP R.7.d.2.3. Arrived 6 P.M.	
TRAPPISTES CAMP	29/4/17		Remained in Camp. Guns cleaned out and checked.	

Reported to top of
7 C - T M B

Army Form C. 2118.

WAR DIARY
or
INTELLIGENCE SUMMARY.
(Erase heading not required.)

Confidential

Original
War Diary
of
176th Light Trench Mortar Battery

From :- 1st Oct 1917
To :- 31st Oct. 1917.

Army Form C. 2118.

WAR DIARY
or
INTELLIGENCE SUMMARY.

(Erase heading not required.)

Place	Date	Hour	Summary of Events and Information	Remarks and references to Appendices
Shaftesbury Camp in the Field	1/10/17	8.30am	Personnel from 1st moved to ISBERGUES. SF 50.55. Belgium to go.	
	2/10/17		Remained in Billets.	
	3/10/17		" "	
	4/10/17		Kit Inspection	
	5/10/17		Bathing.	
	6/10/17		Advance party sent to LISBOURG. Maj. HAZEBROUK 5".	
	7/10/17		Guns & wagons from 1st moved to LISBOURG-LAIRES Road N 7.4 on LISBOURG. Maj. HAZEBROUK 5".	
	8/10/17		Inbuses Lorries etc.	
	9/10/17		General Training. Reserve Battery man out on Exercises, T.M. horses sent back to their units.	
	10/10/17		Battery & Personnel moved to Foss. 10. Corps R.A. LENS II Sh 2. 70x25m	
	11/10/17		Guns sites & ammunition stores checked.	
	12/10/17		Capt. Hempsall reconnoitred new line, held by 1st CANADIANS. Guns sent in relief to relieve Hy. on LIEVIN M345 S.27 four guns taken into the line to relieve 1st CANADIAN LTMB.7. 2 guns left below. Byng Rgd 1203	
	13/10/17		Quartermasters stores moved to GOYEFFLES FARM N.4. Capts R. moved to Dour Hy. on LIEVIN M34.05.27 four guns taken into the line to relieve 1st CANADIAN LTMB.7. 2 guns left below. Byng Rgd 1203	
	14/10/17		Registered on targets. Men engaged on each section in cleaning up the Ground.	
	15/10/17		Nothing unusual to report	
	16/10/17		Third J.B.C.Simpson + N.Stafs Rgt. became attached to this unit for this work. Spent on various targets throughout the day.	
	17/10/17		One Gun T.M. on left sector put out of action. A piece of Shrapnel entering an indentation on the barrel. Caused a split some way [?]. Ships on M. J. Catterman of C., by High & Leading cutting during the day.	
	18/10/17		Fired on same targets sharp all day. Non K. wounded. Gun ? caused a rifle arm covered by tonight.	

Army Form C. 2118.

WAR DIARY
or
INTELLIGENCE SUMMARY.
(Erase heading not required.)

Instructions regarding War Diaries and Intelligence Summaries are contained in F. S. Regs., Part II. and the Staff Manual respectively. Title pages will be prepared in manuscript.

Place	Date	Hour	Summary of Events and Information	Remarks and references to Appendices
Thistle Dump	19/4/17		Nothing unusual to report.	
	20/4/17		Pte F. Ireland wounded. 2nd Lieut R. Ware whilst carrying up posters.	
	21/4/17		Nothing unusual to report	
	22/4/17		Mortar assisted in bath ascents. Sgt Smith proceeded on leave.	
	23/4/17		Preparing ammunition in sections. Commenced digging a pit ever carriage gun pit. One gun in action.	
			225 of ???? ?? Bess left about midday off on Block Type Double Bend 2.2.g 5.7 may 3.	
	24/4/17		Hostile Bd T.M. very active around Thistle Old Hope W.23 a 65 27. Pt Biships wounded in hand not ?????.	
			In Sniffs Pit at M.32.g.1. Bombard posts ? new implacements.	
	25/4/17		Continued work on new implacements	
	26/4/17		Mew cell gel continued work on new implacements.	
	27/4/17		Nothing unusual to report	
	28/4/17		" " " "	
	29/4/17		Relieved by 177 L.T.M.B. Thistle Dump - Sap & Offen ???? Pte Bennett wounded on coming out of line. Sgt Llewellyn Howmiright.	
			??????? 176 ?? B.G.P. H.G. Dey GERVIS around 9.3.30 am 9/4/17.	
	30/4/17		Stay in Billets	
	1/5/17		Kit Inspection. Bathing.	

W. Hempsied Capt.
176 L.T.M.B.

Army Form C. 2118.

WAR DIARY
or
INTELLIGENCE SUMMARY.
(Erase heading not required.)

Place	Date	Hour	Summary of Events and Information	Remarks and references to Appendices
			Original War Diary of 176th Coy. Canadian Machine Gun Battery. From 1st May 1917 to 30th May 1917	London

Army Form C. 2118.

WAR DIARY
or
INTELLIGENCE SUMMARY.
(Erase heading not required.)

Instructions regarding War Diaries and Intelligence Summaries are contained in F. S. Regs., Part II. and the Staff Manual respectively. Title pages will be prepared in manuscript.

Place	Date	Hour	Summary of Events and Information	Remarks and references to Appendices
In the Field	1/11/17		Training carried out during morning as per training programme. Brigade Parade for distribution of medals & G.O.C.'s Inspection.	
"	2/11/17		Training carried out as per programme.	
"	3/11/17		" " " "	
"	4/11/17		Capt. Hempsell, Lieut. Fris & Lieut. Score reconnoitre new line held by 172 T.M.B. (AVION SECTOR). No church parade.	
"	5/11/17		Training as per programme. Lieut. Lane & Lieut. Fris attended lectures at Special Lessons on treatment of Trench feet.	
"	6/11/17		Moved from GUEY SERVINS at 2:00 pm by light railway to Advanced Headquarters at LA COURLETTE, to relieve 178 L.T.M.B. Relief carried out successfully. 4 guns in the line, under command of Lieut. Fris & Lieut. Score.	
"	7/11/17		Nothing unusual to report.	
"	8/11/17		Various targets engaged. Improvements carried out on cellars & gun emplacements.	
"	9/11/17		Work continued on emplacements. Barrage put over for a raid by I/9/5. of Nouveaux.	
"	10/11/17		Gas attack carried out on hostile positions. Hostile Artillery retaliated.	
"	11/11/17		Nothing unusual to report.	
"	12/11/17		Hostile gas shell Bombardment. No casualties.	
"	13/11/17		Hostile gas shell Bombardment on same area as yesterday. No casualties.	
"	14/11/17		Remained of coy sent up to line from LA COULETTE to assist in improving gun emplacements for Coy come guns.	
"	15/11/17		Work on new emplacements proceeded with. Working party from Infantry 30 ammunition. Raid for 17/4/17 cancelled	
"	16/11/17		Four guns drawn out of line with teams & men sent down to GARENCY.	
"	17/11/17		Relieved by 3rd Ays. T.M.B. Proceeded to GUEY SERVINS.	
"	18/11/17		Men cleaned up in Billets.	
"	19/11/17		Left GUEY SERVINS by route march for BERNEVILLE	
"	20/11/17		Remained in Billets.	
"	21/11/17		Left BERNEVILLE for COURCELLES-LE-COMTE.	

Army Form C. 2118.

WAR DIARY
or
INTELLIGENCE SUMMARY.
(Erase heading not required.)

Place	Date	Hour	Summary of Events and Information	Remarks and references to Appendices
In the Field	22/11/17	—	Remained in Billets.	
	23/11/17		Marched to ACHIET-LE-GRANDE entrained for FINS, detrained & marched to HEUDICOURT.	
	24/11/17		Remained in Billets.	
	25/11/17		" "	
	26/11/17		Training as per programme. Officers on tactical Brigade scheme.	
	27/11/17		Moved to RIBECOURT at short notice. Being sling scheme behind.	
	28/11/17		Marched from RIBECOURT to FLESQUIRES to relieve 2nd Guards T.M.B. Captain Stanford & Lieut Price with small party reconnoitre front line BOURLON WOOD. Remainder of men under Lieut Lane & Lieut Senn used by Brigade as carrying party. Five men wounded whilst on party.	
	29/11/17		Remainder of men completed efforts of Brigade by Gas Gun Coy. Shell Bombardment that night. Lieut Senn with thirty men go into hospital. Twenty sixteen men. Ordered by Brigade to stand to & be prepared to resist hostile attack under command of O.C. Recon by 4/6 Leicesters.	
	30/11/17			

R.W. Crawford Capt
O.C. 176 T.M.B.

Army Form C. 2118.

WAR DIARY
or
INTELLIGENCE SUMMARY.
(Erase heading not required.)

Confidential

Original

War Diary
of
116th Light Trench Mortar Battery

from 1st Dec. 1917
to 31st Dec. 1917

176 T.M.B.

Army Form C. 2118.

WAR DIARY
INTELLIGENCE SUMMARY
(Erase heading not required.)

Place	Date	Hour	Summary of Events and Information	Remarks and references to Appendices
In the line	1/12/17	—	In the line at FLESQUIERES	
"	2/12/17	—	"	
"	3/12/17	—	Relieved by the 178 T.M.B. and proceeded to TRESCAULT	
"	4/12/17	—	Proceeded to METZ	
"	5/12/17	—	Pr. METZ to LECHELLE	
"	6/12/17	—	In camp at LECHELLE	
7-9/12/17		—	Training at LECHELLE	
	10/12/17	—	Pr. LECHELLE and entrained at YTRES whence for RUE	
	11/12/17	—	Arrived RUE 5 a.m.	
12-31/12/17		—	Resting at RUE	

O. Evans Lt.
A/Ap 176.T.M.B.

O/C 176.T.M.B.
28/12/17

Army Form C. 2118.

WAR DIARY
or
INTELLIGENCE SUMMARY.
(Erase heading not required.)

Confidential

War Diary
of
the Light Trench Mortar Battery

From 1st January 1918
to 31st December 1918

Army Form C. 2118.

WAR DIARY
or
INTELLIGENCE SUMMARY.
(Erase heading not required.)

Instructions regarding War Diaries and Intelligence Summaries are contained in F.S. Regs., Part II. and the Staff Manual respectively. Title pages will be prepared in manuscript.

Place	Date	Hour	Summary of Events and Information	Remarks and references to Appendices
In the Field	1/1/18		Rest at RUE.	
	2/1/18		" " "	
	3/1/18		" " "	
	4/1/18		" " "	
	5/1/18		" " "	
	6/1/18		" " "	
	7/1/18		" " "	
	8/1/18		" " "	
	9/1/18		" " "	
	10/1/18		" " "	
	11/1/18		" " "	
	12/1/18		" " "	
	13/1/18		" " "	
	14/1/18		Left RUE entrained for LIENCOURT.	
	15/1/18		Arrived LIENCOURT marched to BEAUFORT.	
	16/1/18		Commence Training.	
	17/1/18		Carried out Training Programme	
	18/1/18		" " " "	
	19/1/18		" " " "	
	20/1/18		" " " "	
	21/1/18		Left BEAUFORT for BERLENCOURT by route march arriving 5 p.m.	
	22/1/18		Carried out Training Programme	
	23/1/18		" " " "	
	24/1/18		" " " "	
	25/1/18		Brigade Scheme.	

A5834 Wt. W4973/M687 750,000 8/16 D.D. & L. Ltd. Forms/C.2118/13.

Army Form C. 2118.

WAR DIARY
or
INTELLIGENCE SUMMARY.
(Erase heading not required.)

Place	Date	Hour	Summary of Events and Information	Remarks and references to Appendices
Ch. Th. Dull	26/1/18		Lt BERLENCOURT for MANIN by motor lorrie	
	27/1/18		Church Parade	
	28/1/18		Carried out Training Programme	
	29/1/18		" " " "	
	30/1/18		" " " including Brigade Runs	
	31/1/18		" " " Gunnery practices in IV Corps T.M.School Range	

J. H. Ewin LT
for OC 176 LTM Battery

A5834 Wt. W4973/M687 750,000 8/16 D. D. & L Ltd. Forms/C.2118/13

Army Form C. 2118.

WAR DIARY

~~INTELLIGENCE SUMMARY~~

(Erase heading not required.)

Confidential

Original War Diary
of
176th Light Trench Mortar Battery

From 1st Feby 1918
to 28th Feby 1918

Army Form C. 2118.

WAR DIARY
or
INTELLIGENCE SUMMARY.
(Erase heading not required.)

Instructions regarding War Diaries and Intelligence Summaries are contained in F.S. Regs., Part II and the Staff Manual respectively. Title pages will be prepared in manuscript.

Place	Date	Hour	Summary of Events and Information	Remarks and references to Appendices
In the Field	1/2/18		Carried out Training Programme at MANIN.	
	2/2/18		Bathing Morning. Football Afternoon.	
	3/2/18		No Church Parade.	
	4/2/18		Brigade Route March.	
	5/2/18		Inspection by VI Corps Commander.	
	6/2/18		Firing Practice on VI Corps T.M. School Range. Cleaning guns & overhauling guns & equipment & ready for the line.	
	7/2/18		Moved from MANIN to GRAND RULLECOURT. by Route March	
	8/2/18		" GRAND RULLECOURT to BERLES-AUX-BOIS. by Route March.	
	9/2/18		" BERLES-AUX-BOIS to ARMAGH CAMP. HAMELINCOURT by Route March.	
	10/2/18		Moved from ARMAGH CAMP part of way by bus & remainder by route march to relieve 220 LTMB in Right Section (Bullecourt). Relief carried out peacefully. Mammoth stores moved from ARMAGH CAMP to DUISART CAMP which became Rear Hqrs.	
	11/2/18		Nothing unusual to report. Position of Guns. 3 Mrs in forward position on S.O.S. lines, gun in rear on " Break Through" Emplacements.	
	12/2/18		Nothing unusual to report.	
	13/2/18		" "	
	14/2/18		Hostile Artillery more active. Between 9 pm & 11 pm vicinity of GORRE ALLEY was bombarded with Gas Shells. Thus comm'd.) 382&B Old Darlington 3/11 Staffs Road of Gas Poisoning	6	2223 J 25 Old Darlington (7 J.M. Staffs & Old Darlington | 76 G. Staffs Gassed.)	
	15/2/18		Nothing unusual to report.	
	16/2/18		" "	
	17/2/18		Aerial Activity greater. 2 Hostile Aeroplanes brought down. Hostile planes heard bombing behind our lines between 10 pm & 12 pm.	

A 5834 Wt.W.4973/M687 750,000 8/16 D.D. & L. Ltd. Forms/C.2118/13.

Army Form C. 2118.

WAR DIARY
or
INTELLIGENCE SUMMARY.

(Erase heading not required.)

Instructions regarding War Diaries and Intelligence Summaries are contained in F. S. Regs., Part II. and the Staff Manual respectively. Title pages will be prepared in manuscript.

Place	Date	Hour	Summary of Events and Information	Remarks and references to Appendices
In the Field	18/9/18		Hostile Artillery Active. 2 Hostile Aeroplanes brought down. Hostile planes had bombing in Back Areas between 8 & 11 p.m.	
	19/9/18		New emplacements made at U.29.a.35.15 for offensive guns. One T.M. fired 25 rounds on junction of sunken Reserve & Railway Trench & sunken road in U.29.a.	
	20/9/18		Hostile Gunfire located at U.29.b.00.35. Our T.M's fired 21 rounds at 1.30 p.m., several direct hits were observed on Trench. Nothing unusual to report.	
	22/9/18		Harassing fire now been around emplacements at U.29.d.20.30 & U.29.d.35.30 for offensive purposes.	
	23/9/18		Hostile Artillery very active in NOREUIL VALLEY from 12.30 p.m. to 1.30 p.m. & from 3.30 p.m. to 4.30 p.m. Two new emplacements finished.	
	24/9/18		Hostile Artillery active on NOREUIL VALLEY from 3 to 4 a.m. otherwise normal. At 10.55 pm a light was seen sailing over our lines from direction of the enemy. Probably a balloon fitted with a light as a Wind Indicator. Nothing sufficient known.	
	25/9/18		Everything normal. Nothing to report.	
	26/9/18		Aerial Activity Greater. Hostile plane was seen to crash between Bullecourt & Hendecourt at 11.30 a.m. At 12 noon an Observation Balloon was seen high up anything East to West well to the south of this sector.	
	27/9/18		Hostile Artillery shelled NOREUIL VALLEY & sunken road between NOREUIL - LONGATTE between 3 pm & 5 pm with heavy calibre shells.	
	29/9/18		Hostile Artillery fairly active. NOREUIL VALLEY shelled heavily from 3 pm to 4 am.	

R.H.Hopwood Capt.
O/C 176th Light T.M. Battery.

WAR DIARY

~~INTELLIGENCE SUMMARY~~

(Erase heading not required.)

Army Form C. 2118.

Original

Confidential

War Diary

of

116th Light Trench Mortar Battery

From 1st March 1918
To 31st March 1918

Army Form C. 2118.

WAR DIARY
or
INTELLIGENCE SUMMARY.
(Erase heading not required.)

Instructions regarding War Diaries and Intelligence Summaries are contained in F. S. Regs., Part II. and the Staff Manual respectively. Title pages will be prepared in manuscript.

Place	Date	Hour	Summary of Events and Information	Remarks and references to Appendices
In the Field	1/3/18		In line right sector BULLECOURT. Nothing unusual to report.	
	2/3/18		Hostile Artillery shelled MOREUIL VALLEY & onwards. New emplacements commenced in SHEFFIELD SUPPORT & PUDLEY TRENCH	
	3/3/18		Quiet all day. Nothing to report. Work on new emplacements proceeded with.	
	4/3/18		Our Trench Mortars fired 37 rounds during the night. Work on emplacements proceeded with.	
	5/3/18		Nothing unusual to report.	
	6/3/18		A raid was carried out at 5.35 a.m. on enemy Trenches. 1 M.Gun & 4 prisoners taken. Casualties 2 killed 3 Wounded. Killed A/Cpl F Larkin & Pte. Smith. Wounded A/Sgt J. R. Hopewell, Pte Steele P & Pte Bowring.	
	7/3/18		Nothing unusual to report.	
	8/3/18		Hostile Bombardment in vicinity of sunken road NOREUIL-LONGATTE. Rev. 6 W Barker J. J. wounded	
	9/3/18		" " IGAREE CORNER with H.E. & Gas Shells.	
	10/3/18		Relieved by 17 & 18 & M.B. & moved to DURRAN CAMP. MORY.	
	11/3/18		Guns etc cleaned & checked.	
	12/3/18		Working Party for R.E's. Coat. MORY.	
	13/3/18		Standing to for Hostile Attack	
	14/3/18		Training as per Programme.	
	15/3/18		" "	
	16/3/18		" "	
	17/3/18		Church Parade MORY	
	18/3/18		Baths: Iron Rations Inspection Syphilis	

Army Form C. 2118.

WAR DIARY
or
INTELLIGENCE SUMMARY.
(Erase heading not required.)

Instructions regarding War Diaries and Intelligence Summaries are contained in F. S. Regs., Part II. and the Staff Manual respectively. Title pages will be prepared in manuscript.

Place	Date	Hour	Summary of Events and Information	Remarks and references to Appendices
In the Field	19/3/18		Relieved 177 L.T.M.B. in Bullecourt & left sector.	Ap. Dx
	20/3/18		Nothing unusual to report.	Ap. Dx
	21/3/18		German attack commenced at 5 a.m. Casualties. 5 Missing, 11 Wounded including Lt Sigginthon Wounded	Ap. Dx
	22/3/18		In action all day fired about 100 rounds.	Ap. Dx
	23/3/18		Came out of action & moved to DOUCHY AVETTE	Ap. Dx
	24/3/18		Marched to BOUZINCOURT	Ap. Dx
	25/3/18		" BEAUCOURT	Ap. Dx
	26/3/18		" CANDAS	Ap. Dx
	27/3/18		Remained at CANDAS	Ap. Dx
	28/3/18		Entrained at CANDAS for GODEWIN-LEGAL.	Ap. Dx
	29/3/18		Remained in Billets at GAUCHIN-LEGAL	Ap. Dx
	30/3/18		Received Wire Divisional Commander's compliments on part taken in German attack.	Ap. Dx
	31/3/18		Stores went on in advance to new area.	Ap. Dx

R. Hornet
176 Light Trench Mortar Battery

176th Brigade.
59th Division.

176th BRIGADE LIGHT TRENCH MORTAR BATTERY

APRIL 1918.

Army Form C. 2118.

WAR DIARY
or
INTELLIGENCE SUMMARY.
(Erase heading not required.)

Confidential

Original

War Diary
of
116th Light Trench Mortar Battery

From 1st April, 1918
to 30th April 1918

176th Trench Mortar Battery

Army Form C. 2118.

WAR DIARY
or
INTELLIGENCE SUMMARY.
(Erase heading not required.)

Instructions regarding War Diaries and Intelligence Summaries are contained in F. S. Regs., Part II. and the Staff Manual respectively. Title pages will be prepared in manuscript.

Place	Date	Hour	Summary of Events and Information	Remarks and references to Appendices
In the Field	1/4/18	—	Battery marched to HOUDAIN, entrained for WATOU.	Oft
	2/4/18	—	Carried out training programme WATOU.	Oft
	3/4/18	—	Inspected by II Army Commander.	Oft
	4/4/18	—	Carried out training programme WATOU.	Oft
	5/4/18	—	" " " "	Oft
	6/4/18	—	" " " "	Oft
	7/4/18	—	" " " "	Oft
	8/4/18	—	" " " "	Oft
	9/4/18	—	" " " "	Oft
	10/4/18	—	Marched to POPERINGHE. Entrained for YPRES. Billeted in GENDARMIERE	Oft
	11/4/18	—	Relieved 102nd L.T.M.B. PASSCHENDAELE Sector	Oft
	12/4/18	—	Quiet-use day. Came out of line to VLAMERTINGHE.	Oft
	13/4/18	—	Left VLAMERTINGHE and marched to RENINGHELST.	Oft
	14/4/18	—	Left RENINGHELST for LOCRE.	Oft
	15/4/18	—	Left LOCRE, Relieved 147th L.T.M.B. BAILLEUL	Oft
	16/4/18	—	Withdrawn from BAILLEUL & took up position N.W. of BAILLEUL with 147th Bde.	Oft
	17/4/18	—	Attack on line by enemy at 3:30 pm. frustrated by French. Wounded Lt. GRICE P.L.	Oft
	18/4/18	—	GREATRIX, MARRIOTT, DUTCH. Have since been relieved at night by 147th L.T.M.B Battier or WESTOUTRE	Oft
	19/4/18	—	Left WESTOUTRE for TEDMERDEN	Oft
	20/4/18	—	Left TEDMERDEN for ELVERDINGHE dist.	Oft
	21/4/18	—	Left ELVERDINGHE for OOSTCAPPEL	Oft
	22-23/4/18	—	Carried out training program at OOSTCAPPEL	Oft
	24/4/18	—	Left OOSTCAPPEL for line West of POPERINGHE	Oft
	27/4/18	—	took up positions on SWITCHLINE between RENINGHELST and OUDERDOM	Oft
	28/4/18	—	2nd Lieut. FOREMAN killed	Oft
	29/4/18	—	" " " "	Oft
	30/4/18	—	" " " "	Oft

R Long Capt.
9/5/18 L.T.M.B.

Army Form C. 2118.

WAR DIARY
or
INTELLIGENCE SUMMARY.
(Erase heading not required.)

Place	Date	Hour	Summary of Events and Information	Remarks and references to Appendices

Instructions regarding War Diaries and Intelligence Summaries are contained in F. S. Regs., Part II. and the Staff Manual respectively. Title pages will be prepared in manuscript.

CONFIDENTIAL

WAR DIARY
of
176 TRENCH MORTAR BATTERY

From :- June 11th 1918
To :- Aug 31st 1918

Volume I.

WAR DIARY
INTELLIGENCE SUMMARY

Army Form C. 2118.

Place	Date	Hour	Summary of Events and Information	Remarks and references to Appendices
Nabrius	11.		176 Jewel Mortar Battery proc. formed. The [illegible] arm came from the Rails in the Rot. 18. 135 & Bm. EngRs. Spot Ass. 2 in. St. M. & [illegible] The 3 Inf Rails in the Royal Sussex.	Roger
		12 NOON	The Corps General Inspecting the Battery.	Roger
		12.30	Moved the Battery under Captain C.G. Burden to NON VALE village.	Officer
		1.30	Arrived at 2.30 pm village	Rogers
		4.30	Myster [Speen?] & C.O.S & M in Command [illegible] Grumman	Rogers
GUERNON VAL 17			BATTERY. Organisation duties remaining. Officers moved billets.	Officer
	13	9.30	Inspection of Battery by Captain Co.	Officer
			Rolloff with Umaros in rink. Officers inspection of [illegible]	
			PARADE 6.5 Eating from 9 am to 3 pm. Tuition of Battery Personnel	
	15.		BATTERY Organisation & Training	Rogers
	15.			Officer
	17.			
	17.	9.30		Officer
		12.1		

Army Form C. 2118.

WAR DIARY
or
INTELLIGENCE SUMMARY.

(Erase heading not required.)

Instructions regarding War Diaries and Intelligence Summaries are contained in F. S. Regs., Part II. and the Staff Manual respectively. Title pages will be prepared in manuscript.

Place	Date	Hour	Summary of Events and Information	Remarks and references to Appendices
GUERNONVAL	22		[illegible handwritten entries]	(1) Appx
		7.15am	Battalion to prepare to move and evacuate huts.	(2) Appx
			Order to move was cancelled.	(3) Appx
		9.45pm	Gas N.C.O. from Bde reported to S.G.R.S. and artillery gas bde to be round on Friday.	(4) Appx
		D.Y.S	Raided heavily	
		11.30	Batteries burst [illegible] ordered a detail to PSYVES Hall	(5) Appx
		5.30	Pull Len TALBOT ADLIVER + Lt. P. LOM 13th and Lieut. of Piquet	(6) Appx
			ordered ran.	(7) Appx
			Hot dinner for the military of First [illegible] turn to bile	(8) Appx
			Received [illegible] orders that [illegible] for billets to move BEAUMOURT as untilled Battn	(9) Appx
	23	7.30am	[illegible] J.H.K drew [illegible] Maps to BEAUMOURT	(10) Appx
		8.30	Battn. [illegible] moved off from FERNIVAL via [illegible]	(11) Appx
			[illegible] which was billeted on outskirts of town	(12) Appx
			Arrived at BEAUMETZ-LES-LOGES	(13) Appx
		1.45	Moved off to BIZZCOURT [illegible] arrived at [illegible]	(14) Appx
			[illegible] Battn. [illegible] [illegible]	(15) Appx

WAR DIARY
or
INTELLIGENCE SUMMARY.

Army Form C. 2118.

Place	Date	Hour	Summary of Events and Information	Remarks and references to Appendices
BRETENCOURT	24	9.30 am	Captain G.G. BULMAN visited the line MEGGATT SECTOR	Cpt Capt
		5.30 am	GOGIDIN (59th) Inspected the Battery might march to BRETENCOURT	A/Capt
				A/Capt
	26	8.15	Captain C.G. BULMAN visits NM TALBOT & N LORD in 2nd R B (?)	A/Capt
			returned to BLAIREVILLE QUARRY	C/R Capt
		4 pm	Passed over a RIDGE	
			Sent forward to ORS and 2nd Lt NM TALBOT & 2nd Lt NN LORD	B/Capt
			No HQ Place ment to to to the Reserve in Coy positions SMAy	
		DK 10.55	SGT. TMR. TOOK Captain G.G. BULMAN and 2nd Lt NN LORD	
			round PURPLE LINE to inspect and all the gun positions	A/Capt
			and Rifle Pitts formed	
		9.30pm	HOLMES relieved thousand frames of BRETENCOURT	A/Capt
			on Company march up	
	27	1.08	Captain not being of party joined 2/6 TWRs and 70 TWRs	A/Capt
		7.15	P/o C.Q. WALKER 108473 accidently shot wound from 9/65th RWF	CR/Capt
	28	10.9. am	Relieved 2/6th LN TALBOT NJ and 2/6th LORD	B/Capt
			Deaths 381860 killed	A/R Capt

Pte FRAZER 416797 wounded

Place	Date	Hour	Summary of Events and Information	Remarks and references to Appendices
	29.	AM 11.00	Pte GASKELL wounded. Pte Bradway's Knife also bruises to arms	CR Copy/1
			W⁹ Cowan 436469 " " " wrist & 4ft " hip. No cas.	CR Copy/1
		PM 9.30	Relief was not continued until 9.30 PM. No cas.	
			6 unwounded returned from Gassey there 4 rather casualties	CR Copy/1
	30.	PM 5.45	Captain C.G. Bulman reported to B.S.S. Hqrs No 176 – E.S.O. No 3 Bde 4 Brigade	CR Copy/1
			C.G. BULMAN Taking the line.	Second.
	31.		Captain C.G. BULMAN firing on the line to new 6.S. gun positions	
			RH View G 4 the RED line	
				CR Bulman Capt
				OC 176. TMB

Army Form C. 2118.

WAR DIARY
or
INTELLIGENCE SUMMARY.
(Erase heading not required.)

ORIGINAL
Confidential

War Diary
of
175 Trench Mortar Battery

From 1.8.18.
To 31.8.18
Volume II

Army Form C. 2118.

WAR DIARY
INTELLIGENCE SUMMARY.
(Erase heading not required.)

Instructions regarding War Diaries and Intelligence Summaries are contained in F. S. Regs., Part II. and the Staff Manual respectively. Title pages will be prepared in manuscript.

Place	Date	Hour	Summary of Events and Information	Remarks and references to Appendices
BLAIRE-VILLE MER CATEL Sector	1	5.30 pm	2nd Lieut H. R. Sutton by Shaw Qual Highland returned to relieve 2nd Lieut G. H. LORD	(C.B.Capt)
	1-2		OC 178 TMB. OC 177 TMB. Reports at HAN FARRANGE Affair.	a.O.8H
			Relief 2-3.	
	1	5 pm	OC 177 TMB toured the posts & is unable the above gun positions easy by wire from WRETON COURT	
	2	am	Lieut G. H. LORD proceeded to BARBY accompanied by Lieut J. A. JAKEO and started inspecting Limpers to find the best way of finding	(C.L.Capt)
		10 AS	gun ammo ......to char Nauge	
			Wire 177 + 178 T.M.Bs	
	3		The relief was complete 18/19. Last sent west 10 AM were the	(C.Reng)
			Sections under 2nd Lieuts JACOB, FELLOWES with the line. One they	
			and WM arrived in 13A HIC = V.h.5 QUARRY until after 12 noon	a Report
			5 ORs left BLAIRE VILLEMER CATEL arriving at BARBY and proper the Picardian	C.L.Capt)
			Station CL Suleer Qual J. A. TAKEO in Bray. making a 3.35am	
			K. S. R. + K. W. R. + Lieut J. H. Ibb .... at .... brought along with	(C.Capt)
			....K. R. T. JOW-EN-ARTOIS. Lieut CARLISLE also was on the post	
4	1 AM	Voluntary Church Service.	
1/18		Battery formed for Rifles and received a clean change	R.O.H.
5 pm		Pm.	

Army Form C. 2118.

WAR DIARY
or
INTELLIGENCE SUMMARY.

(Erase heading not required.)

Instructions regarding War Diaries and Intelligence Summaries are contained in F. S. Regs., Part II. and the Staff Manual respectively. Title pages will be prepared in manuscript.

Place	Date	Hour	Summary of Events and Information	Remarks and references to Appendices
BARLY	5	9 am	Battery had Kit Inspection; Ammunition and Shells cleaned	Rt. Cpt
	6	9 am	By. training under O.C.; arrangements	Rt. Cpt
		2 pm	Range firing with dummies	
	7	8 am	Test morning order received from Brigade. G.S. wagons loaded, additional stores stocked ready for travelling and all ready to move off at 9.30 am	Rt. Cpt
BLAIRVILLE MERCATEL SECTOR.	8	2 pm	By. training and fired on Range with dummies Relief 1st R.L. M.B. Bty & 500 (MERCATEL) 2 Sugs. + 2 Subaltern entered Front line 1st Lt. P Infantry Support to	Rt. Cpt
	9			Rt. Cpt
	10			Rt. Cpt
	11		2nd Lieut returned to Bde	Rt. Cpt
	12		Capt R. Baine arrived to take over Bty/141 from Capt E.D. Meara 2nd Lt Ladkin admitted to Hospital	Rt. Cpt
	13		Fairly quiet, nothing of importance to report	Rt. Cpt
	14		2nd Lieut. Copps left Battery to report at Employment Base Depot Etaples	Rt. Cpt
	15		Fairly quiet, nothing of importance to report Fired 36 rounds into By Scope in this Sector at M.36 & end	Rt. Cpt

Army Form C. 2118.

WAR DIARY
or
INTELLIGENCE SUMMARY.
(Erase heading not required.)

Instructions regarding War Diaries and Intelligence Summaries are contained in F.S. Regs., Part II and the Staff Manual respectively. Title pages will be prepared in manuscript.

Place	Date	Hour	Summary of Events and Information	Remarks and references to Appendices
BLAIRVILLE - MERCATEL SECTOR	16		Capt Dishman left Battery and reported unit 2nd Lt H W Roland arrived	Lt Cpt
	17	10.30pm	Fired 32 rounds Harassing fire with Hyrde Sap	Lt Cpt
	18		Constructed two new gun positions in front line	Lt Cpt
	19		G.O.C. visited front line & inspected gun positions & H Qrs	Lt Cpt
	20/21	12 pm - 6.35 am	Shoot to in support of Infantry Action. Gun position S.5.b.05.95 E.30.a 35.00	Lt Cpt
	21		Inter Battery chip both places	Lt Cpt
	22/23		Advance of the 52nd Div through our lines	Lt Cpt
	23/24	9.30 pm	Bns relieved upon completion of four hours duty in Line. Marched to Ballard Val Bivouacker in field at 2 AM	Lt Cpt
	24	6 am	Proceeded to Saulty by road arriving 7 AM rested side of railway whilst awaiting transport entrained 5pm for billets passed night in Train delayed slightly by air Raid at St Pol	Lt Cpt
	25	5 AM	Arrived billets Bonniere 2nd Lt Rowland & 4c Hedgemen proceeded forward to billets St Hilaire Bytles	Lt Cpt
	26	5.30 am	Received order to move Advance Horse Billets 6 pm by road Battery moved off at 3pm to A584 of W1973/M687 950690 8/16 D.D. & L. Ltd. Forms/C.2118/13. billets H H Line by march route	Lt Cpt

Army Form C. 2118.

WAR DIARY
or
INTELLIGENCE SUMMARY.
(Erase heading not required.)

Instructions regarding War Diaries and Intelligence Summaries are contained in F. S. Regs., Part II. and the Staff Manual respectively. Title pages will be prepared in manuscript.

Place	Date	Hour	Summary of Events and Information	Remarks and references to Appendices
HAMEL BILLETS	27	9am	Battery training under BC's arrangements	R Sgt
		11.30a–5pm	R.A. Inspection in afternoon	
			PAY.	
	28	9–11.30a	Battery training under OC's arrangements	R Sgt
	29	9–12.30p	Battery training under OC's arrangements afternoon Park & change of Underclothes	O Cpl
	30	9–12.30p	Battery training & dismounted firing under OC's arrangements	B Cpl
	31	9–12.30p	Battery training & crossing & dummy firing under OC's arrangements	B Cpl
		5.25p	Received heavy order & S wagon packed & ready to move off 6pm	
		6.45pm	Arrived Asylum St Vincent	

R S Cpl

O/c 173 - T. M B

Army Form C. 2118.

WAR DIARY
or
INTELLIGENCE SUMMARY.
(Erase heading not required.)

War Diary
of
176 Light Trench Mortar Battery

Confidential

From 1-9-18
to 30.9.18

Volume III

Army Form C. 2118.

WAR DIARY
or
INTELLIGENCE SUMMARY.
(Erase heading not required.)

Instructions regarding War Diaries and Intelligence Summaries are contained in F. S. Regs., Part II. and the Staff Manual respectively. Title pages will be prepared in manuscript.

Place	Date	Hour	Summary of Events and Information	Remarks and references to Appendices
Asylum ST VENANT	1st		Situation quiet nothing of importance to report Battery standing by	RL opt
	2	9 am	Moving orders received. 12 Noon Battery inspected by 1/112 Infty order to move commenced	RL opt
	3	11 am	Order to move off deferred. Standing period Pb t 20.6.0. Left Asylum 12.30 pm	RL opt
		4.45 pm	Relieved 177 LTMB at Q4 c 40.50	RL opt
Calonne	4	9.0-11.30pm	Battery collected Sahbags + Tools. 9pm Nos1 mount out arrived at Bretell's R 15 d 37 95	RL opt
		9pm	Placed 6 Guns teamsier positions Nos 1+2 at B.21 c 70.90 Targets Bridge + Road R21 t	RL opt
			and Bridge + Road R.15 d 25.90. Nos 3+4 at R.10 d 10.80 Targets Bridge R19 d 05.10	RL opt
			and Bridge + approaches R9 t 90.10, Nos 5+6 Guns at R4 d 55.65 Targets Bridge R3 t 95 25	RL opt
			and Bridge R9 a 15 95	RL opt
	5		Battery Standing by nothing orders to move forward. Situation Quiet, nothing of importance	RL opt
			to report	RL opt
	6		Capt Lewis + Dr Barker reconnoitred line and Gun positions. Battery remained standing	RL opt
			by awaiting orders	RL opt
	7	1 pm	1pm Received orders to move 3 Guns arrived off Gun belts arrived at Reid HQ. to 12 t 25 30	RL opt
			Convoy R2 c 4.5 pm	RL opt
	8		Situation quiet nothing of importance to report	RL opt

Army Form C. 2118.

WAR DIARY
or
INTELLIGENCE SUMMARY.
(Erase heading not required.)

Place	Date	Hour	Summary of Events and Information	Remarks and references to Appendices
LESTREM	9	1pm	Received orders to move forward & relieve 174 Bde. Arrived at 4.0. WANGERIE & pd Bde Hd Qrs U.S. & Co to relieve completed 2 AM. nothing of	R2. Ont
	10		importance. Nwd. shelled and directed some pressure. Enemy further preparations to report	Ont
	11		Quieter day. Nothing of importance to report	Ont
	12	9 am	Relieved 45 Bde into Div. Rest Area to the West of the LA BASSEE Canal. Relief completed	Ont
			A N 13 b 95 25. Relieved by Div'l Artillery N.S. a	Ont
	13	10.15	Received BAby order to proceed to sidings & move sic D.27 relieving arti	Ont
			Battery came away so two hrs early left at spur running in siding	Ont
		10.30pm	had relief of guns ready to move R.12 C 20 35	Ont
			Capt Boyd & 2/L Ranken S. recoursed reported anticipating good Billetting.	Ont
	14		anywhere in report	Ont
			Lieut W.G.B. & lot Men took up Advance Guns Position.	Ont
	15		Battery served as Programme. R.12 C 20 50. Nothing further worth reporting. Some planes	Ont
	16		in sight.	Ont
	17		Battery turned no performance. Nothing of enemy Aircraft	Ont
	18		Battery took part in Tactical movement. Nothing of any great interest to report	Ont

Army Form C. 2118.

WAR DIARY
or
INTELLIGENCE SUMMARY.
(Erase heading not required.)

Instructions regarding War Diaries and Intelligence Summaries are contained in F. S. Regs., Part II. and the Staff Manual respectively. Title pages will be prepared in manuscript.

Place	Date	Hour	Summary of Events and Information	Remarks and references to Appendices
	19	9-12.30p 2-4pm	Battery fired under 2.J's covering movements Battery wiped over line posts and of Duthorlizer	M. OH R. OH
	20	2.30– 9.30	Battery fired batteries and close strict supp to battery 230-12.30p Artillery training	R. OH Q. OH
	21	2pm	No movements 2pm fired 50 rds practice at long range at Hem	Q OH
	22		Battery turned on infantry movements Situation quiet nothing of importance to report	B OH O OH
	23	9-12.30p	Battery fired 50 rds practice M2.C. 10. 00	O OH
	24	9-12.30pm	Battery training under Q.6.10 engagements	Q OH
	25	9-12.30	Battery fired 30 rds M2C 10.00	Q OH
	26	9-12.30	Battery training Archery layed Drill re Ditto	R OH Q OH
	27	9-12.30		O OH
	28	9 am 7 pm	Received orders to take part in attack to take place on the 30th Officers went forward to front line with a portion of the N.C.O's to select gunpositions for the purpose of assisting with the barrage. Returned to Batty HQ + sent forward a N.C.O with a party to receive ammunition at DEAD END ROAD.	R OH Q OH R OH R OH R OH R OH

Army Form C. 2118.

WAR DIARY
or
INTELLIGENCE SUMMARY.
(Erase heading not required.)

Place	Date	Hour	Summary of Events and Information	Remarks and references to Appendices
	29	6.30 am	Went round to gun positions chosen 3 in GREAT NORTH ROAD	R. Oct
		12 m. mid-night	TRENCH, 2 in PICCADILLY TRENCH, 1 in WINDY POST. Dug the gun pits with the assistance of a carrying party supplied by 147 Brigade carried up 45 rds per gun, which was detonated in gun pits.	R. Opt
R. Opt
R. Opt
R. Opt
	30	7.30 am	Lt. Lees opened fire on the selected Targets for 20 minutes	R. Opt
		10 am	510 rounds were fired. Left the guns in position and withdrew ammunders as instructed out of area of gas proposed to be sent over by gas projectors.	R. Opt
R. Opt
R. Opt
		3 pm	Billets were shelled at RED HOUSE and DEAD END ROAD The following were wounded by shell fire #2159 A/Cpl Kynan D. 27309 Pte Kirk, 5728 Pte Thomas. #2892 Pte Mount, 205911 Pte Skilton says Pte Edwards 30927 Pte Bent sent them to SUSSEX R.A.P. All were sent to B.D.S.	R. Opt
R. Opt
R. Opt
R. Opt
R. Opt

R.O. Cpt
R. Cpt L.T.M.B.
O/C No 174 L.T.M.B.

ORIGINAL

Army Form C. 2118.

WAR DIARY
or
INTELLIGENCE SUMMARY.
(Erase heading not required.)

Confidential War Diary
76 L.T.M.B.

From 1st Oct
to
31st Oct 1918

Place	Date	Hour	Summary of Events and Information	Remarks and references to Appendices

Instructions regarding War Diaries and Intelligence Summaries are contained in F. S. Regs., Part II. and the Staff Manual respectively. Title pages will be prepared in manuscript.

Army Form C. 2118.

WAR DIARY
or
INTELLIGENCE SUMMARY
(Erase heading not required.)

Place	Date	Hour	Summary of Events and Information	Remarks and references to Appendices
LAVENTIE	1	9400	Reported with 2 guns to each front line Battalion, 2 left Bnky with	Cpl. Cpt
			guns to 25th K.R.R. on left & 2 2/Lt Rowland with 2 guns to 17th R.S.R. on right	2/Lt
			Gun positions dug & assist with barrage for attack at 4.30am	Cpt
			2/Lts 2 guns in GREAT NORTH ROAD on right & 2/Lt Bnky 2 guns in PICCADILLY	Cpt
			TRENCH on left sector firing for 5 mins on special targets	Cpt
			enemy being during night of 1st/2nd at intense Long-ration	Cpt
			of trenches at No.1 Post. Last burst of fire carried ammunition	Cpt
			with assistance from carrying parties (men) from R.S.R.	Cpt
	2	0001	Completing gun positions to the locating hosts. Bombed Hostile	Ht
			Posts pt 63 y75 Lizies bank which arrived at RED HOUSE 0130	Cpt
		0500	Proceeded to gun positions & completed the location of bombs.	Cpt
		09.30	& assisted to give with Lewis gun with barrage on left sector of Brigade	Cpt
			front. Third Ly with our guns the attack was successful	Cpt
			they were held up on the attack at 50 3rd Lr advanced No.1 up &	Cpt
		12.40	Two guns on left advanced & took up 50 5th Lr advanced No.1 up &	Cpt

Army Form C. 2118.

WAR DIARY
or
INTELLIGENCE SUMMARY.
(Erase heading not required.)

Instructions regarding War Diaries and Intelligence Summaries are contained in F. S. Regs., Part II. and the Staff Manual respectively. Title pages will be prepared in manuscript.

Place	Date	Hour	Summary of Events and Information	Remarks and references to Appendices
LAVENTIE	2		and N30a4.0. Two guns on right relieved	R. OM
		15.00	Received instructions to hand over gun positions to 144 S.T.M.B. at 15.00	R. OM
SAILLY SUR 3		03.00	Relief completed and teams returned to RUE VERTE	R. OM
LA LYS 4		12.00	Battery embussed at M5.a.4.0 and proceeded to S.y.35	R. OM
			and took possession of billets.	R. OM
	4	10.00	Received instructions to relieve 140 S.T.M.B at I.14.a.30.M.	R. OM
		14.30	Battery embussed at S.y.35 proceeded to the gorse.	R. OM
		18.00	4 Gun teams left at a.g.n.25. proceeded to I.14.a.30.M. to relieve	R. OM
			140 S.T.M.B.	R. OM
		21.00	Relief completed.	R. OM
	5	08.00	H.Q left Haggards proceeded to I.14.c.3.0ff. + made H.Q.	R. OM
	6	08.00	Carrying parties proceeded up line with Rations + ammunition	R. OM
			during the day	R. OM
	7		Nothing of importance to report	R. OM
	8	09.30	— " —	R. OM
	9	08.00	Ammunition carried up line + not much doing day	R. OM

Army Form C. 2118.

WAR DIARY
or
INTELLIGENCE SUMMARY.
(Erase heading not required.)

Instructions regarding War Diaries and Intelligence Summaries are contained in F. S. Regs., Part II. and the Staff Manual respectively. Title pages will be prepared in manuscript.

Place	Date	Hour	Summary of Events and Information	Remarks and references to Appendices
ARMENTIERES	10.	01.00	Parties proceeded up line with ammunition - shot snipers during day	12 OR
FRONT			day	4 OR
	11.	10.30	31 Rounds fired at snipers post in village	2 OR
		R.O.R	Carrying parties proceeded up line with ammunition & shot sniper	2 OR
	12.	09.40	20 Rounds fired at house in village believed snipers post	2 OR
		14.00	Ammunition + one gun taken to late of line	2 OR
	13.	10.30	35 Rounds fired into wood at enemy gun limbers	2 OR
		12.00	Ammunition + gun much taken up line	2 OR
	14.	09.45	Sept. Line ammunition and limbers up by gun teams	2 OR
		11.40	Guns left withdrawn to rest billets	2 OR
		4.00	Incupposition dug 3rd position near barricade cancelled	12 OR
			owing to front line tube being withdrawn	2 OR
	15.	09.00	Teams stood by awaiting orders	2 OR
	16.	08.10	Left hand ammunition billets for Legume	2 OR
		09.30	+ own G ammunition advanced to I.33 a 60.40	2 OR

WAR DIARY or INTELLIGENCE SUMMARY

Army Form C. 2118.

(Erase heading not required.)

Place	Date	Hour	Summary of Events and Information	Remarks and references to Appendices
ARMENTIERES/16				
FRONT	17	10.45	H.Q.s advanced to I.14.d.40.60.	2 Ox
		8.30	Guns + ammunition advanced 800yds to support advance	1 Ox
LILLE		10.00	" " to Witternes + Villelers	2 Ox
			ab 4.30h in bivouac by canal	d Ox
		16.00	H.Q.s advanced to Chateau VILLERS	d Ox
	18		H.Q.s moved to St Andre + met guns halted by side of canal	2 Ox
		14.40	returned across canal + billeted for night in Lomelette	2 Ox
	19	05.00	Guns + H.Q. advanced until 9.30.	2 Ox
BHADS		13.30	advanced to 20.60.10.75 billeted for night	2 Ox
	20	09.00	Steady advance, Capt. Stone went forward for billets	10 Ox
		14.00	advanced to ARLEUX-etc.	8 Ox
	21	09.30	Capt. Stone reconnoitred gun positions	8 Ox
		12.10	Battery advanced to Escopliere etc.	d Ox
		17.15	Guns + ammunition taken up to position in Marsh	d Ox
			village covering lantern bridge	4 Ox

Army Form C. 2118.

WAR DIARY
or
INTELLIGENCE SUMMARY.
(Erase heading not required.)

Instructions regarding War Diaries and Intelligence Summaries are contained in F. S. Regs., Part II. and the Staff Manual respectively. Title pages will be prepared in manuscript.

Place	Date	Hour	Summary of Events and Information	Remarks and references to Appendices
TEMPLEUVE	22	09.00	Nothing important to report	R, O.R
		12.00	Received notice of relief by 1/7 S.W.B.	R, O.R
		17.00	Relief by 1/7 S.W.B. completed	R, O.R
		20.30	Arrived in billets in HERSEAUX	R, O.R
	23	09.00	Nothing of importance to report	R, O.R
	24	06.00	Training under O.C. arrangements	R, O.R
	25	"	do	R, O.R
	26	"	do	R, O.R
	27	11.00	Church Parade	R, O.R
	28	09.00	Training under O.C. arrangements	R, O.R
		12.30	do	R, O.R
	29	—	do	R, O.R
	30	—	do	R, O.R
	31	09.00	Brigade Parade. General's inspection & presentation of ribbons	R, O.R
		10.30		R, O.R
		12.00	Gas drill & cleaning guns	R, O.R

Confidential

War Diary
176 L/M.B

From 1st November
to
30th November 1916

Original

Army Form C. 2118.

WAR DIARY
or
INTELLIGENCE SUMMARY.
(Erase heading not required.)

Instructions regarding War Diaries and Intelligence Summaries are contained in F. S. Regs., Part II. and the Staff Manual respectively. Title pages will be prepared in manuscript.

Place	Date 1918 Nov	Hour	Summary of Events and Information	Remarks and references to Appendices
TOUFFLERS	1	09:00	Training under OC's arrangements	Pt Cpt
"	2	09:00	Training under OC's arrangements	Pt Cpt
"	3	09:00	Training under OC's arrangements	R Cpt
"	4	09:00	Training under OC's arrangements	R Cpt
"		10:30	Battery ordered to stand-by for moving	R Cpt
"	5	09:00	Battery standing-by	R Cpt
"	6	09:00	"	R Cpt
"		10:00	Moving orders cancelled. Training resumed	R Cpt
"	7	09:00	Battery took part in Jacket scheme	R Cpt
"		11:00	Returned to billets	R Cpt
"	8	09:00	Battery standing by	R Cpt
"		14:45	Battery marched to TEMPLEUVE	R Cpt
"		16:45	arrived at TEMPLEUVE	R Cpt
			178 L.T.M.B. (Map 37. H33 & 60:00)	R Cpt
TEMPLEUVE	9	11:00	Marched from TEMPLEUVE to ST. AUBERT via billets from TEMPLEUVE & ST AUBERT	R Cpt

Army Form C. 2118.

WAR DIARY
or
INTELLIGENCE SUMMARY.
(Erase heading not required.)

Instructions regarding War Diaries and Intelligence Summaries are contained in F. S. Regs., Part II. and the Staff Manual respectively. Title pages will be prepared in manuscript.

Place	Date	Hour	Summary of Events and Information	Remarks and references to Appendices
ST AUBERT	9.	20.45	Arrival at ST AUBERT. hit meal served (Map 47 I 10 b 00.25)	R. Cpt.
-"-	10.	09.00	Left ST AUBERT	R. Cpt.
VELAINES	-"-	10.00	Arrived at VELAINES billeted in concrete hall (K 13 c 50 50)	R. Cpt.
-"-	11.	09.00	Battery standing by. Orders that exercise commenced 11.00 h	R. Cpt.
-"-	12.	09.30	Marched from VELAINES (K 13 c 50 50) To (I 10 b 00.25)	R. Cpt.
ST AUBERT	-"-	12.40	Arrived at ST AUBERT. Rep 37 L 18 L 00 25	R. Cpt.
-"-	13.	09.00	Dummy and fancy until 12.30 h	R. Cpt.
-"-	14.	09.00	Training until 11.00 h	R. Cpt.
-"-	-"-	11.30	Battery to leave new headquarters at Hotel Belle Vue (map 47 M 5 d 6c 10)	R. Cpt.
-"-	15.	10.00	Marched from ST AUBERT	R. Cpt.
WILLEMS	-"-	16.00	Arrived at WILLEMS (Map 37 M 5 d 6c 10)	R. Cpt.
-"-	16.	09.45	Marched from WILLEMS (Map 37 M 5 d 00.10)	R. Cpt.
LILLE	-"-	14.30	arrived at LILLE (Map 36 Q 15 c 30.20)	R. Cpt.
-"-	17.	09.00	Inspection cloth + clothing	R. Cpt.
-"-	18.	09.00	Training under 9/6 arrangements	R. Cpt.

Army Form C. 2118.

WAR DIARY
or
INTELLIGENCE SUMMARY.
(Erase heading not required.)

Instructions regarding War Diaries and Intelligence Summaries are contained in F. S. Regs., Part II. and the Staff Manual respectively. Title pages will be prepared in manuscript.

Place	Date	Hour	Summary of Events and Information	Remarks and references to Appendices
LILLE	19	09.00	Training under O/Cs arrangements	H Oft
-"-	20	09.00	Training under O/Cs arrangements + Educational training	H Oft
-"-	21	09.00	Training under O/Cs arrangements + Educational training	H Oft
-"-	22	09.00	Training under O/Cs arrangements + Educational training	H Oft
-"-	23	09.00	Training under O/Cs arrangements by 1 pm	R Oft
-"-	24	09.30	Barrack Parade - Distribution of Medal Ribbons by	H Oft
-"-			Lt. Gemmel - Church Parade	N Oft
-"-	25	09.00	Training under O/Cs arrangements + Educational training	H Oft
-"-	26	09.00	Training under O/Cs arrangements + Educational training	H Oft
-"-	27	09.00	Training under O/Cs arrangements + Educational training	R Oft
-"-	28	09.00	General Holiday	H Oft
-"-	29	09.00	Training under O/Cs arrangements + Educational training	H Oft
-"-	30	09.00	Training under O/Cs arrangements + Educational training	H Oft

Near Oft

of H L T M R

Original

Army Form C. 2118.

WAR DIARY
or
INTELLIGENCE SUMMARY.
(Erase heading not required.)

Instructions regarding War Diaries and Intelligence Summaries are contained in F. S. Regs., Part II. and the Staff Manual respectively. Title pages will be prepared in manuscript.

War Diary
September
from 1st Dec 1918
to 31st " 1918

196 S.T.M.B.

Place	Date	Hour	Summary of Events and Information	Remarks and references to Appendices

Army Form C. 2118.

WAR DIARY
or
INTELLIGENCE SUMMARY.

(Erase heading not required.)

Instructions regarding War Diaries and Intelligence Summaries are contained in F. S. Regs., Part II. and the Staff Manual respectively. Title pages will be prepared in manuscript.

Place	Date Dec	Hour	Summary of Events and Information	Remarks and references to Appendices
LILLE	1st	09:00	Church Parade. (Map ref 9.15E. 80-22)	M. O/S
	2nd	09:00	Training under O/C's arrangements & Educational Training	" O/S
	3rd	09:00	Training under O/C's arrangements & Educational Training	" O/S
	4th	09:00	Training under O/C's arrangements & Educational Training	" O/S
	5th	09:00	General Holiday	" O/S
	6th	09:00	Entrained at Rd 8-157 arrived at Barlin	" O/S
BARLIN	7th	13:30	Billeted at Meze 22-10.	" O/S
		09:00	Repairing Huts &c	" O/S
	8th	10:00	Hut Inspection	" O/S
	9th	09:00	Training for Inoculation	" O/S
	10th	09:00	Searching for Ammunition	" O/S
	11th	09:00	Searching for Ammunition	" O/S
	12th	09:00	General Holiday	" O/S
	13th	09:00	Training under O/C's arrangements & Educational Training	" O/S
	14th	09:00	— do —	" O/S
	15th	10:00	Church Parade	" O/S

Army Form C. 2118.

WAR DIARY
or
INTELLIGENCE SUMMARY.

(Erase heading not required.)

Instructions regarding War Diaries and Intelligence Summaries are contained in F. S. Regs., Part II. and the Staff Manual respectively. Title pages will be prepared in manuscript.

Place	Date Dec	Hour	Summary of Events and Information	Remarks and references to Appendices
BARLIN	16	09.00	Training under the arrangements of Battalions Comdg	
	17	09.00	Training under the arrangements of Battalion Comdg	
	18	09.00	Training under the arrangements of Battalion Comdg	
	19	09.00	General Holiday	
	20	09.00	Training under the arrangements of Battalion Comdg	
	21	09.00	Training under the arrangements of Battalion Comdg	
	22		Church Parade	
	23	09.00	Training under the arrangements of Battalion Comdg	
	24	09.00	Training under the arrangements of Battalion Comdg	
	25		Xmas Day Church Parade	
	26	09.00	General Holiday	
	27	09.00	Training under the arrangements of Battalion Comdg	
	28	09.00	Training under the arrangements of Battalion Comdg	
	29	09.00	Church Parade. Special Thanksgiving Service for news	
	30	09.00	Training under the arrangements of Battalion Comdg	
	31	09.00	Training under the arrangements of Battalion Comdg	

Major OC 1/7 M.R.